SMART CONTRACTS

THE ESSENTIAL GUIDE TO USING BLOCKCHAIN SMART CONTRACTS FOR CRYPTOCURRENCY EXCHANGE

By Jeff Reed

© Copyright 2016 by Jeff Reed. All rights reserved.

This document is geared towards providing exact and reliable information in regards to the topic and issue covered. The publication is sold with the idea that the publisher is not required to render accounting, officially permitted, or otherwise, qualified services. If advice is necessary, legal or professional, a practiced individual in the profession should be ordered.

- From a Declaration of Principles which was accepted and approved equally by a Committee of the American Bar Association and a Committee of Publishers and Associations.

In no way is it legal to reproduce, duplicate, or transmit any part of this document in either electronic means or in printed format. Recording of this publication is strictly prohibited and any storage of this document is not allowed unless with written permission from the publisher. All rights reserved.

The information provided herein is stated to be truthful and consistent, in that any liability, in terms of inattention or otherwise, by any usage or abuse of any policies, processes, or directions contained within is the solitary and utter responsibility of the recipient reader. Under no circumstances will any legal responsibility or blame be held against the publisher for any reparation, damages, or monetary loss due to the information herein, either directly or indirectly.

Respective authors own all copyrights not held by the publisher.

The information herein is offered for informational purposes solely, and is universal as so. The presentation of the information is without contract or any type of guarantee assurance.

The trademarks that are used are without any consent, and the publication of the trademark is without permission or backing by the trademark owner. All trademarks and brands within this book are for clarifying purposes only and are the owned by the owners themselves, not affiliated with this document.

Table of Contents

Introduction 1

CH1: Smart Contracts 101 3

CH2: Solidity and Smart Contracts 21

CH3: Dapp Setup 29

CH4: The State of Affairs of Smart Contracts 33

Conclusion 43

Additional Resources 45

Introduction

Today, smart contracts are becoming popular in the e-commerce industry. Although relatively new, a lot of people are seeing the potential of this technology. Smart contracts are being used in small processes today, but it is easy to see how beneficial smart contracts will be on a larger scale. Smart contracts can easily replace lawyers for online transactions. Every little detail and every little change made to the contract is being documented. This is like having a digital recorder of all the things surrounding your processes. And since everything is automated, information is up to date and it is very unlikely that the information will be tampered with.

Smart contracts are still in the infancy stage. It has not gained a lot of supporters, but it is showing a lot of potential. There is not much proof of its effectiveness on a larger scale but its peer to peer interactions are producing a lot of promise. Through these small interactions, smart contracts are being acclaimed as among the top breakthrough innovations of today's generation. By buying a copy of this book, you are giving yourself full access to everything you need to know about smart contracts and how this technological breakthrough can impact your life.

This book is guaranteed to help you understand the basics of smart contracts and how it works. You can also gain the knowledge on how you can make the most out of this very promising technology. The practical uses of smart contracts are enumerated in this book and you will also learn how you can make your own smart contracts in the Ethereum system. You will also get tips on how you can make your smart contacts easy to understand and user-friendly. This book also covers some of the myths surrounding smart contracts and the reasons why they exist. There are also explanations disproving these myths.

You can now explore the wonderful world of smart contracts, through this book, and see for yourself how it can change the way you are doing business online. You can certainly find practical uses of smart contracts for yourself and in a larger scale of things. Smart contracts can be maximized once tried on a large scale business or in government practices. Once you start using smart contracts, it may be difficult for you to go back to the old ways.

CH1

Smart Contracts 101

Smart contracts are referred to as the next level of the blockchain platform. And since blockchain is an important aspect of smart contracts, it is just practical to discuss what a blockchain is before we dig in deeper into what a smart contract is. A blockchain is a scattered database with an ever expanding list of records, or blocks. These blocks are stored on different hard drives scattered around the world. The hard drives are referred to as the nodes. The blockchains are automatically updated every time information is put in the chain. This automation guarantees that the information on the chain has minimal to no error. The overlapping of the nodes protects the blocks from being revised or being tampered with. The nodes are designed to make the system virtually indestructible and extremely secure. A blockchain acts as a ledger for all public transactions. Blockchain technology is discussed in detail in *Blockchain: The Essential Guide to Understanding the Blockchain Revolution.*

Your Guide to Smart Contract Basics

Blockchain technology is a very compelling technology. A lot of users give so much reverence to this technology; they see blockchain technology equally important as the internet. Blockchains were used primarily to transmit financial data. In reality, blockchain technology can perform several complex commands efficiently. Blockchain technology can determine how many bitcoins your digital wallet has. It is in this regard that smart contracts come into play. Smart contracts play a huge role in blockchain enterprise applications. Smart contracts will most likely be the leader in blockchain technology in the years to come. They serve several intangible benefits that our technology is experiencing today.

A smart contract is automatically activated after a program or command has been completed. A block will be given to this smart contract and it will become a part of the chain. To put it simply, a smart contract can be compared to that of a debit card. The owner, or a third party authorized by the owner, can make automated deductions on your checking account whenever you use your debit card. Smart contracts work in almost the same manner. The only difference is that it works in a decentralized way because its hard drives are situated in different locations around the world. A smart contract is a type of computer code that records when and how the changes are made in the contract.

When a smart contract is performed in a public blockchain, no third party can stop the transaction from happening. As with the debit card example, the bank can act as the third party who can influence what happens to the account. But smart contracts discount the idea of third parties. Smart contracts can execute on their own without the influence of a third party. For this reason, the transaction is deemed extremely secure. However, it is important to note that even with the presence of a third party, or a blockchain, the transaction is just as secure. This is because of the decentralized system that it makes it impossible to hack a blockchain.

As discussed earlier, a blockchain acts as a public ledger. Smarts contracts that are carried out using a blockchain can be seen by anyone who has a copy of the chain. These contracts are readily available for public consumption so there is no room for discussion or debate. You cannot question the terms of the contract or its results. A smart contract is simply a record of the facts as they happen. It is in this nature that smart contracts can be viewed as a good thing or a bad thing, depending on the information that is made available to the public.

Traditional vs. Smart Contracts

Traditional tangible contracts created by professional legal practitioners rely heavily on third parties to reinforce what is on the contract. These contracts are written in legal language that involves an enormous amount of paperwork. This type of contract does not only consume a huge amount of time, but it can also turn out to be very ambiguous. The ambiguity stems from the fact that not all of us understand the legal language in which these contracts are written. Law practitioners prepare the contract and enforce them accordingly. If contracting parties do not agree on the terms of the contract or in the way each of them acted, the public judiciary system will resolve the issue for them. Once this happens, more resources will be spent as this process costs so much and it is very time-consuming.

Smart contracts are generally set up by computer programmers using smart contract programs and development tools. Smart contracts are completely digital, which means there is not a lot of paperwork involved in the process. They are written in binary programming codes and these codes dictate the terms and consequences of the contract. The language is easy to understand because there is not much technical legal system jargon. And unlike traditional contracts, a third party is not necessary for the enforcement of the contract.

Types of Smart Contracts

Financial Services. Cryptocurrency has spawned several different applications of smart contracts. For example, smart contracts can administer auctions without the need for third-party entities to enforce the rules of the auction. Smart contracts can take simple binary codes and translate them into commands that the system can perform. The system can point out the highest bidder of the auction and award the auctioned item accordingly, and return everyone else's money all at the same time. This kind of efficiency is what makes smart contracts very promising.

Property Law. Cryptocurrencies such as ether and bitcoin can be used to trade digital assets on a one-dimensional blockchain. Cryptographic techniques are put in place to ensure that the owner of a digital coin will be the only one to spend it. This principle can be related to electronically-controlled physical products embedded with microchips.

Credit Enforcement. Credit enforcement is an extension of the property law. It is a typical example of how smart contracts can be applied in the real world. Smart contracts can be created to disable your account whenever you fail to make payments. Take your credit card account as an example. If you are not able to make a payment on your monthly credit card bill and you already exceeded your card limit, then your account will be suspended until such time that you are able to make the payment.

Breach Prevention. Smart contracts are especially useful in the music and video industry. Digital Right Management technology prevents you from unauthorized use of music and videos that are protected by copyrights. A public blockchain has the ability to track copyrights for each music or video. Every time a music or video is used for commercial purposes, the copyright owners will receive royalty payments. Smart contracts can also set the terms as to how the payment should be split between the performers, songwriters, and producers. And since the information is available in public blockchains, we know that it had not been altered.

Double Deposit Method. BitHalo and BlackHalo were some of the pioneers of the double deposit method. The idea is fairly simple, but the results are very powerful. Double deposit method is designed for the trade of cryptocurrency. The double deposit method works in such a way that when two parties try to cheat on each other, both of them will lose the same amount of what they should have earned. The program does not attempt to determine which party did not perform his side of the bargain; it merely ensures that parties who do not come to an agreement at the specified time limit will be penalized for it. This persuades both parties to come to a resolution or they will both lose what they have.

Oracle Contracts. Since smart contracts rely heavily on the data that is being inputted in the blockchain system, it may be hard to tell what really happened in the physical world. It may be difficult for smart contracts to determine who is telling the truth when it comes to the actual situation. To solve this problem, oracle contracts were created. Oracles can get information from external sources which can be used as a source of data for smart contracts.

Smart Contracts Across Different Industries

Smart contracts are becoming very prominent in the financial industry. This is mainly because of the fact that smart contracts make a lot of contract terms more efficient and simplified. Smart contracts allow users to update the terms of their contracts whenever they want to and they can do it in real time. This is a very far cry from the experience of having to make the same changes to a tangible copy of a contract. It could take several days because of the several back and forth requirement the contract needs to go through to complete the same tasks. Users are thankful because of the speed and hassle-free transaction. In addition, inaccuracies are being minimized since the contract does not have to go through several different channels.

Smart contracts also allow its users to automatically activate their contracts once several preset conditions have happened. Although this may not be very useful to those who do not use it frequently, businesses who do transactions with other businesses will find this greatly valuable. A lot or resources will be saved and the contracting businesses are guaranteed of the security of their transaction. Businesses can also now transact without the use of third parties, thus easing the cost of the contract on both sides.

Financial institutions can also find great uses of the smart contracts. Smart contracts can automatically close out transactions relating to transfers, settlements, and trades once the preset conditions are met. Smart contracts can also be utilized with coupon payments and they can be used to restore the principal for expired bonds. Insurance companies can also use smart contracts to simplify the workflow and minimize errors across different departments. Smart contracts also helped in developing the Internet of Things regulation services.

The health care services also share the same advantages as with the other service sectors.

Medical records can be automatically and accurately updated as patients transfer from one department to another. Information made available in the blockchain can be used to watch over the health of the population, using information that is automatically updated in real time. Participants who joined the public blockchain can be paid automatically (again, through smart contracts) for using their information. Smart contracts can also verify the achievement of fitness goals and give rewards in accordance with the Internet of Things mechanism.

The music industry is using smart contracts to track song usage royalties and awarding payments correspondingly. Information can be added to public blockchains which are add-only databases. This ensures the authenticity of the information since it cannot be altered.

Smart contracts are also being used on transactions between two individuals. This could eventually lead to increase in lending opportunities and energy credits trading.

Real estate can also expedite transactions as there will be less paperwork and the contract is available to both contracting parties. Once the seller and the buyer agree on the terms of the contract, they can digitally sign the contract, transfer the payment from buyer to seller, and turn over the ownership to the buyer. All this can be done online and without the aid of a third party.

The Tesla electric car also adapted the use of smart contracts to automatically bill car users every time they charge their cars at any of their charging stations. Car users can view the record of their bill as smart contracts are updated automatically.

The supply chain industry can also gain seamless shipping experience with the use of smart contracts. Shipments are being automatically documented at various points in the manufacturing, shipping, and delivery process. In cases when there are complaints about the shipment, the whole process can be reviewed and the area where the discrepancy occurred can be traced. This is possible since the delivery went through the same channel where the contract was created.

The insurance industry can also use smart contracts to determine who is liable for every car accident after several conditions have been met. Smart contracts can be used to charge rates according to the operating conditions of the car. There will be minimal disagreement as information is recorded and the contract will be automatically activated once all the conditions have been met.

Smart contracts can also be used to smoothen out the voting procedure. Smart contracts can determine the identity of the person before it gets recorded in the system. Voters' information is kept safe and is unlikely to be tampered with because of the great security that smart contracts provide. When a record needs a closer inspection, it can be easily pulled up from the system for review.

Smart Contracts in the Financial Sector

Smart contracts are a single ledger system that allows the program to easily verify the accuracy of any given information. Smart contracts, when properly executed, can reduce errors and lags in the system which will permit the flawless execution and verification of each project. It also greatly reduces the time of completion of a project and the costs associated with it.

The financial sector can be transformed to reflect security, transparency, efficiency, cost reduction, and innovation. Smart contracts can carry out record keeping and auditing functions, as well as custodial tasks usually done by third parties. The omission of third parties could clearly reduce the cost of transaction for both contracting parties.

Clearing trades are intensively manual in terms of processes. They require a lot of work hours and they even demand a few reconciliations inside and outside of the trading industry. To make it worse, every time reconciliation is made, chances of error also increase. These errors could lead to future additional delays that are more costly and requires the use of extra resources. By using smart contracts, the clearing trade process is smoothened out and the process is simplified tremendously.

Every step in the process is recorded and automatically updated. With the great number of clearing trade transactions made each year, the market is totally ready to adapt this process.

Since the smart contract is a single ledger process; it allows multiple processes in any industry to run smoothly. Most delays usually happen due to physical documentation done during production. A smart contract allows the product to go through all the steps without too much disruption and it can run smoothly. This will greatly improve the process no matter what type of industry it is. Smart contracts can also manage bills and credits from the production of the manufactured goods until the delivery to the customer.

The transaction systems available today cost a fortune. A lot of key players in almost every industry are looking for ways that they can integrate smart contracts into their business. The old-time monitoring system could cost as much as 10 billion US dollars every year. This is a very great motivation for businesses to move their business from being old-fashioned, to adapting the smart contract technology. In the long run, businesses can save a considerable amount of money through this shift in their business practices.

Current Limitations

Blockchain is the future of database system with the smart contract as its front-runner. It is extremely important for businesses that are planning to implement this system to study its uses and prepare for its execution. It is also up to these businesses to encourage other companies to adopt this system. Looking at all the uses of smart contracts, it is hard to think of its limitations as they are immensely outweighed by their uses. But to help you make that decision, there are some points you need to consider before venturing out in the smart contract process.

A lot of smart contracts today are performed in small and medium scale businesses. Smart contracts had not penetrated transactions that are of high volume so they are utterly untested in these environments. Before smart contracts reach the mainstream, the public needs to see them in larger scale transactions where they can be tested and they can prove their potential.

Smarts contracts cannot access information that is not stored in its blockchain system. Oracles are used as access points to external information. However, the best way of embedding oracles in smart contracts is still under discussion. Traditional decentralized networks usually experience approximately 20 seconds of delay. Since smart contracts belong to the decentralized system, it can experience the same delay with the use of oracles. Traditional servers that are in place today can complete the same task in milliseconds.

There are very few examples of the uses of smart contracts in the actual world. The world needs to understand how smart contracts work and give it a chance so it can prove its true potential. In addition, blockchains store information in such a way that once it has been written, it cannot be amended or added as these actions are not part of its base program. In this regard, mistakes cannot be tolerated even during the learning process. This is a major deterrent for smart contracts to capture the public's interest, especially if they are not intended to be used for long-term projects.

Most importantly, smart contracts do not completely adhere to privacy. This is where traditional contracts stand superior as compared with smart contracts. Although smart contracts stored on private blockchains may not have this problem, smart contracts that are made on public blockchains are readily available to all those who are in the blockchain. All the details of the contract are made public to all those who have access to the contract. This poses great risks for the individual users and businesses. As with any other contract, there is some information that contracting parties would not want to reveal to everybody in the thread. If this is not resolved, the use of smart contracts cannot be expected to increase anytime soon.

CH2

Solidity and Smart Contracts

Blockchain technology was first intended to be used with the bitcoin cryptocurrency. However, most smart contracts today are done with the aid of the Ethereum platform. Ethereum is a blockchain-based public platform that makes a virtually decentralized machine. This machine can carry out smart contracts among individuals using ether as their cryptocurrency. This chapter will focus on discussing how smart contracts are able to link up to the Ethereum blockchain. There are different types of blockchain. However, it does not matter what type of blockchain you are connected to; the general processes across different blockchains will always stay the same.

Important Terms

Public key cryptography. Public key cryptography is a two-part scheme comprised of a private key and a public key. Private keys are used by individual users to create a virtual signature which is connected in their blockchains. The public key is used by other users to verify signatures related to the said blockchain. To put it simply, the owner of the private key is sending out public keys to other users so they can gain access to the smart contract that has been created. It is impossible to retrieve the private and public keys externally so it is imperative for the users to set up backups for their keys.

Ethereum virtual machine. Basic bitcoin blockchains only allow basic contracts and cannot accommodate a myriad of steps. The Ethereum Virtual Machine (EVM) makes smart contracts capable of doing more complicated and more powerful contracts.

Dapp. Dapp, also known as a decentralized application, uses smart contracts that are in the

Ethereum marketplace. It can be accessed from any Ethereum node or from a central location.

Getting Started

An Ethereum node is not required for every smart contract but it is recommended for learning exercises. Java, Haskell, C++, and Python are programming tools that can be used to connect to the Ethereum platform. Solidity is a programming tool that is very much similar to JavaScript. This is the most popular way to connect to the EVM using a node. Solidity is devised to collect codes that will run in the EVM. It has an extension of .sol or .se. when connecting to an Ethereum network, a compiler is also necessary. However, etherchain.com offers an alternative to a compiler. Web3.ja is the last item that you will need. Web3.ja is an Application Program Interface (API) that is used to make Dapps.

You can take advantage of open frameworks by using Truffle. A Truffle is a framework of distributed application. Truffle covers most of the fundamental functions of programming and gives individual codes more emphasis. For testing purposes, you can use BlockApps.net. BlockApps.net does not have its own Ethereum node; it only imitates the effect of a real node.

Contracts are not universal across all transactions. However, some points in a contract exist in another contract. Smart contracts are triggered once a set of conditions are met. Set of conditions are usually answered by yes or no, as for how most binary systems work. These conditions are set and modified before the contract is laid out. One of the most important parameters to creating smart contracts is to identify at which point and what circumstances will activate the contract.

The address of your Ethereum wallet is one of the main variables in creating smart contracts. When a contract is activated, a unique address will be generated which is separate from the address that you created. However, this unique address is still associated with the creator's address.

Determining the size of your contract is the next variable that you need to consider. As a rule of thumb, it is better to have smaller and simpler contracts. An oracle will be used to pull up outside information for the smart contract. You need to set the parameters of the information that the oracle will pull up and the location where the information will be lifted from.

Getting Into Details

Your contract should include the information it needs to store and how those parameters can be met. You will need to create a general structure for your contract using the list of parameters that you have prepared. You can use a 2 x n mapping, where n represents the number of parameters of your contract. Each parameter will include definite details that will trigger the activation of the contract.

Using the information, you have outlined in your contract, you will need to incorporate the creator of the transaction and the amount of the contract. You will also need to show the data and mapping information. Your template should be able to map your contract based on the stored integer that labels your contract automatically based on a template.

After completing all the steps above, you need to define the specific tasks your contract will need to perform and the triggers of your contract. The individual who created the contract can send proposer transactions. Under the proposer transactions, you will need to stipulate contract limits, account information of the contracting parties, and other prerequisites to completing your contract.

Investors can create transactions with a unique ID that they can send to the account that had been defined. The storage space will list this transaction in the contract and add it to the total results. A suicide action is triggered when a final transaction has been generated. This action will prevent the contract to be activated again after it has been completed.

During this time, the recipient of the contract can decide how to draw out the accrued funds from the contract. You can create a dummy account and apply yourself under the investor group after the results have been tested. Once you are inside the dummy account, you can dictate how the contract will push through.

Running Things Smoothly

Truffle can assist in making the process more manageable, especially if you are edgy on creating a contract without trying the code first. Truffle aids in the composing stage by allowing you to test the different parameters using a Java-based framework. You need to take note that when verifying transactions, it can take up to 10 seconds under favorable circumstances.

Truffle will require you to have access to the console window and a new client node before you can open the program. Then you can install Truffle so you can create the basic parameters of the contract. You can use the code you have generated to test the program for errors.

Moving On

Once you have generated the code of your contract, you can use the compiled code in the blockchain. You can go to Etherchain.org/solc to compile the code for Solidity. Once your code has been transformed into a useable format, you can set up the cost of the contract in ether cryptocurrency. The program will ask you to sign in using your private key and you will be provided with the unique blockchain address where your contract is located.

To make your contract go live, you will need to use the Truffle program to access the directory where your contract is located. You have to open the Truffle command and then you can access the new directory through the init command. After you have created a new directory under the .sol extension, you will need to enter config/app.son in the program and add your contract in the resulting space. Then you just need to restart Truffle and then run a tesrpc command before installing Truffle at the root directory level. After performing all these steps, your contract should begin exist.

CH3

Dapp Setup

Your contract will need a user interface before you can use it to interact in real time. The Dapp will include an HTML-based front end and a database that will connect you to the Ethereum network. Dapp will connect directly to the Truffle program because it has a complete CDN access and network. The Dapp UI will be created in a similar fashion as that of a website.

Dapp Creation

Truffle is the best program to use when creating Dapp as it will compile your UI after you complete your Dapp's creation. In the Truffle directory App, you simply add your Dapp and run your Truffle again so it can compile all the information in your contract. You also need to remember to register changes in the Build folder so you can reload it in emergency cases.

You will need to find background images in the directory labeled App. You will also need JavaScript and several stylesheets and indexes. You can personalize your contracts based on your requirements by adding codes and getting your frontend UI option running. Once you open the app.js file, a section will popup that contains a greeting from Truffle. Launching this console will show you all of the active commands.

You need to remember all your commands. You also need to create an operation that you can access every time you load your page. You can add window.onload operation in the apps.js file to do this. When executed correctly, this operation will send different account information to the browser console. To ensure that your program is working accurately, you can use the test.conference.js function. This function should show you the balance amount, the balance after an increase, and the total after the account is suspended.

After creating the app.js and the index.html, you should test it on your node or on a sample node that can return results in a timely manner. It should include a form of communication that lets your users know that the results are ready. This is important as the results do not turn out quickly.

You can use the following geth codes as a suggestion.

geth --rpc --rpcaddr="0.0.0.0" --rpccorsdomain="*" --mine --unlock='0 1' --verbosity=5 --maxpeers=0 --minerthreads="4"-networkid'12345'-genesis testgenesis.json

Entering these codes will generate two new accounts labeled as 0 and 1. You need to create passwords for both of these accounts and you may also need to generate a .json test-genesis file which will be categorized in the .json file as "alloc". Using geth codes will require you to account for your ether cryptocurrency. Ether is the currency used in Ethereum. To get a closer look at Ethereum, you can read *Investing in Ethereum: The Essential Guide to Profiting from Cryptocurrencies*. Lastly, you will need to go to the Truffle app folder for all the results. You need to recompile and set up the results of your contract.

SilentCicero recently created an option for Dapp programs to generate a UI. This can be found in DappBuildermeteor.com and it can make HTML codes that can be modified for contracts made on Solidity, Web3.js, or JQuery. This tool does not run as smoothly as you would like it to. However, this is a great alternative if you are still not confident with your skill level and you would prefer not to generate the program on your own. Using the same steps provided above, you can generate a UI. However, if it is not successful, then you can generate a secondary version.

CH4

The State of Affairs of Smart Contracts

Although smart contracts mostly find its uses in hypothetical scenarios, they are believed to be able to solve most of the problems of the online industry today. While they are theoretically able to make transactions flow smoothly, it is not an omniscient entity that can do all things. Below are some of the things that you need to consider when engaging in smart contracts. These things are regarded as smart contract myths that you need to put to rest as of the moment. But who knows, these myths might come true one day as smart contracts continue to progress.

Smart Contracts Legally Bind Contracting Parties

Smart contracts make the automation of small processes possible. However, even when these processes are usually tied with contracts that are legally binding, legislation regarding the legality of smart contracts as an entity is not yet in place. Smart contracts are usually clauses in traditional legally binding contracts and they define the ways in which a transaction should occur. You cannot dispute the stipulations laid out by smart contracts as they only point out the facts of the transaction. It simply tells you whether the stipulations are followed or not.

Even if smart contracts are not formally legislated to be binding contracts, the digital signature attached to every transaction can be enough proof that the contracting parties agreed to enter into some form of arrangement. It is then the responsibility of the contracting parties to follow the stipulation laid out in the smart contract as some jurisdiction may accept them as legally binding. The consequences of breaking a smart contract may be judged in a case to case basis. But to stem away from involving the courts in smart contracts, a solicitor can use information on the contract to come up with an agreement that both parties can abide by. In this manner, small misunderstanding may be fixed without having to go to court.

Smart Contracts are a Form of Ricardian Contract

A Ricardian contract can be used both in the court of law and a software application. The purpose of a Ricardian contract is to protect the digital trading system by means of providing legally binding rights on properties. In this way, contracting parties can concentrate on the opportunities of their business by requiring everyone to honestly and fairly communicate in the digital trade.

As with smart contracts, they are not a form of Ricardian contract. However, smart contracts act as a supplement to Ricardian contracts. Smart contracts simplify Ricardian contracts by using the stipulations on smart contracts as a basis for the

Ricardian contracts. A Ricardian contract also requires a few signatures. It is in this manner that a smart contract becomes valuable. When entering a smart contact, a digital signature is required. You can track the results of the contract by using the digital signatures of the contracting parties.

Smart Contracts Can Be Enforced Legally

There is no legislated law that makes smart contracts legally enforceable. Although pieces of information surrounding a smart contract can be used in courts, it has not been made legal yet to use the entirety of a smart contract as proof for legal action. Results from a smart contract can be used as trails of information that can either support or oppose a statement.

Smart Contracts Have a Mind of Their Own

Smart contracts are binary codes that are designed to determine the status quo and activate the contract once the predetermined terms have been met. Smart contracts, even those that are accessible through oracles, are nothing but circumstance-driven data. A smart contract is driven by preset parameters. It is not in any way a form of artificial intelligence that can act on its own.

Smart Contracts Are Easy to Set Up

The answer to this myth can go both ways. Yes, smart contracts are easy to set up. This is especially true if you are using a smart contract language, like Solidity, in writing your contracts. However, oracles can also be used in creating smart contracts. Oracles are more advanced smart contract programs that have the ability to send a myriad of actionable data to smart contracts.

Smart Contracts Can Only Be Set Up by Developers and Computer programmers

As of today, smart contracts are created by developers and computer programmers as they require an in-depth understanding of how binary codes work. But there are several entry points that will make smart contracts more user-friendly to businesses and individual users. Once this is made possible, smart contract users can create a graphical user interface or a text-based language input. The creation of the browser Ethereum Mist is a step for businesses to move in that direction.

Smart Contracts Are Not Safe

Smart contracts are relatively safe even with the implementation of the Ethereum. Smart contracts run in complete quasi-Turing programs. This only means that contracts are concluded after their execution and there is no risk of repeating the contract infinitely.

Smart Contracts Are Solely Intended for the Use of the Financial Sector

A lot of smart contracts today are tied up with the financial sector. This is one of the reasons why most people think that smart contracts are made solely for this sector. Smart contracts can be used in other industries as well. As mentioned above, smart contracts can also be applied to health care services, music industry, manufacturing, and shipping industry, and it can be potentially applied to make the voting process easier.

With the emergence of the Internet of Things, smart contracts applications have become infinite. Smart contracts bring in trust and transparency to the Internet of Things. The Internet of Things allows business engagement. This is done by making technological resources as potential services that can be traded in the open market in real time, without incurring additional fees.

Businesses Are the Only Ones Who Can Benefit From Smart Contracts

While it may be true that business entities are the first ones to benefit from smart contracts, discounting the fact that smart contracts can be used in our personal affairs is unacceptable. The only reason why smart contracts are still not a part of our personal lives is because not all of us are familiar with it. Smart contracts can be used among peers and neighbors. It may be used in small negotiations like the tradeoff of personal financial favors. Smart contracts can also trigger negotiations along the line of paying for regular goods by allowing one of the contracting parties to set up a repetitive smart contract once the parameters of the transactions have been met.

Smart Contracts Are Designed to be Linked to Other External Factors

Although oracles had been used to connect smart contracts to external nodes, this does not mean that smart contracts can be used to interpret variable conditions in the environment. Smart contracts will remain to be binary codes that rely on the occurrence of a specific set of events. If these set of events do not take place, then a contract will not be laid out. In addition, putting in supplementary variables may throw your results off. This is because two different nodes will most likely return two entirely different results. This could happen in the real world especially that the results will be coming from two different nodes via the oracle. And the 10 seconds delay in getting your results is also a big factor in the variance of your results.

Smart Contracts Can Be a Means to Guaranteeing All Types of Payments

While payments can be made through smart contracts, it is important to note that the payment's string of commands should be embedded within the blockchain where your smart contract belongs. If the payment string does not exist in your blockchain, then it will be extremely difficult to accept and initiate payments through smart contracts. For smart contracts to have the ability to enforce payments, it should be within the bounds set in the blockchain. Not being able to embed the payment strings to your smart contracts will cause your funds to be locked up for prior use. Several transactions may not actually happen because of the distributed system of smart contracts.

Smart Contracts Can Conceal Data

This may still stand true with a private blockchain. However, public blockchains have the tendency to make information available to all those who have access to it. This can pose a danger to individuals and to business entities. Not all contacting parties would like to have the information of their contracts available for everybody to see. As of the moment, there are several efforts to make some sections of the blockchain undecipherable to others.

Conclusion

Congratulations on making it to the end of *Smart Contracts*! This book was meant to inform and explain the fundamentals of smart contracts. My hope is that your knowledge of smart contracts has increased. If you wish to learn more about financial technologies check out the following *Additional Resources* section!

Additional Resources

Other books, by Jeff Reed, on Amazon:

- *Investing in Ethereum: The Essential Guide to Profiting from Cryptocurrencies*

Available in Kindle, audiobook, and paperback form.

- *Blockchain: The Essential Guide to Understanding the Blockchain Revolution*

Available in Kindle, audiobook and paperback form.

- *Fintech: Financial Technology and Modern Finance in the 21st Century*

Available in Kindle, audiobook and paperback form.

Check out Jeff Reed's other books on Amazon:

http://bit.ly/JeffReedBooks

www.ingramcontent.com/pod-product-compliance
Lightning Source LLC
Chambersburg PA
CBHW070522210526
45169CB00027B/1174